The Maple City Rubber Company

100 YEARS AND GROWING

Kieth A. Peppers and Thomas Kubat

Commoner Company · Cleveland

Copyright 2015, Maple City Rubber Company

All rights reserved.

Published by Commoner Company, LLC
Cleveland Ohio

ISBN-10:098564740X
ISBN-13:978-0-9856474-0-7

All photos credited to Maple City Rubber Company,
unless otherwise labeled.

Dedicated to the families of Claud V. Martin Sr., Charles Switzer and the past, present and future employees of the Maple City Rubber Company.

Acknowledgement

We would like to acknowledge all of the following, without whom this book could not have been produced: Michael Kilbane, Paul Bennett, Claude Martin Jr., Kenneth Spaar, Karen Rosales, Claudia Simons, Tom Wireman, Jack Brock, Diana Slauterbeck, Lynn Duchez Bycko, Matt McNeely, Keith Mundorff, the Norwalk Historical Society, Huron County Recorders Office, and Pursue Posterity (with a very hardy thanks to Keirston Swope).

The Copyright Office of the United States of America certifies that registration of a claim of copyright for two copies of the "print or pictorial illustration" of children playing with balloons, as shown in the above rendering, was made in the name of the Maple City Rubber Company on January 15, 1925.

FULL SERVICE BANK
Kroger
BURGER KING
HOME OF THE WHOPPER
things go better with Coke
COTTON'S
HOLSUM
BREAD
SANTA
Easter SHOE PARADE
YOUR AD COPY HERE
good hands with ALLSTATE
YOUR AD COPY GOES HERE
MARATHON
YOUR AD COPY HERE
YOU'LL LOVE JONES FOODS
SACHS Quality
YOUR SALES MESSAGE OR LOGO HERE

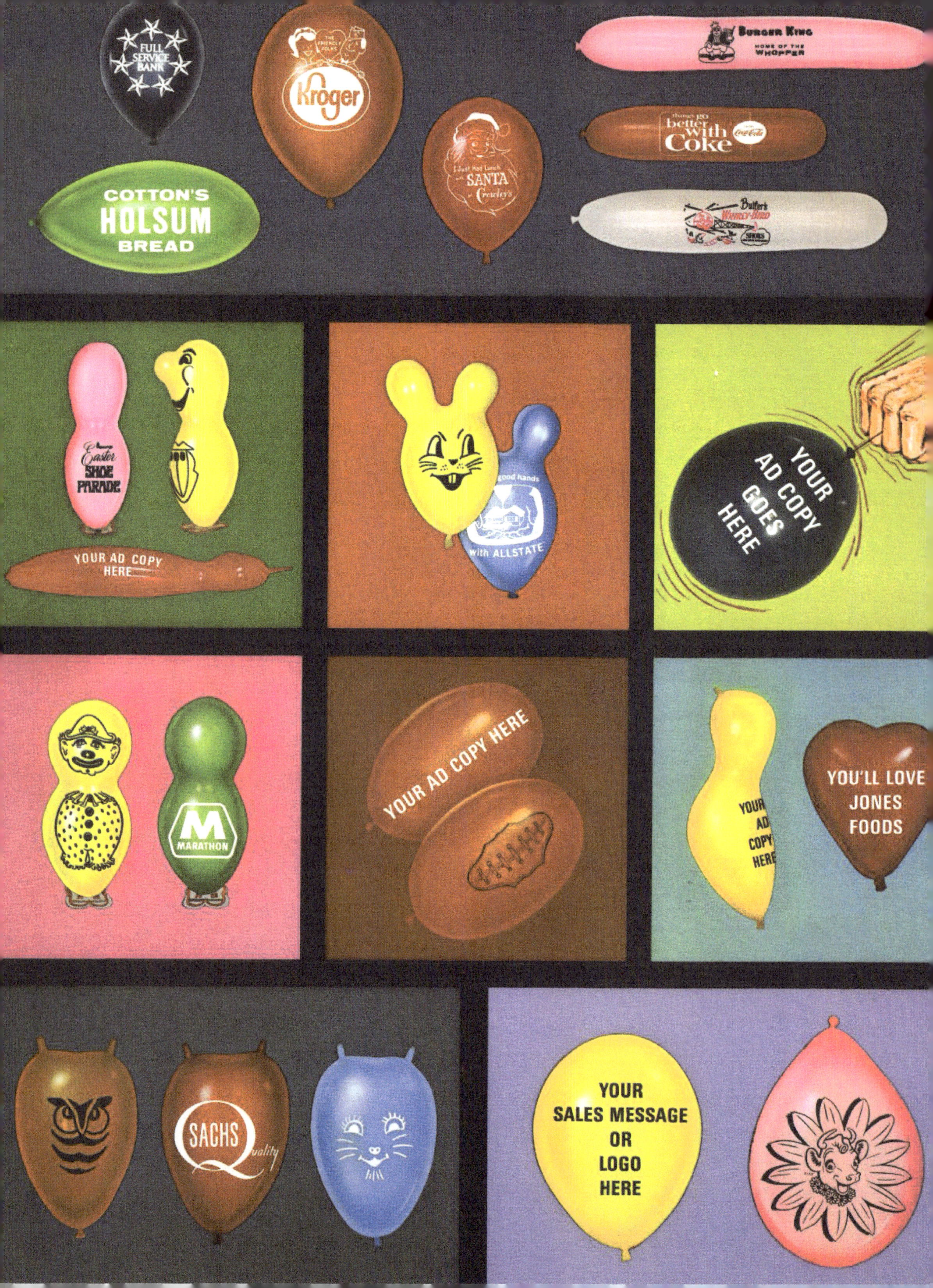

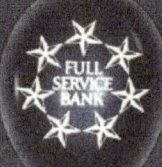

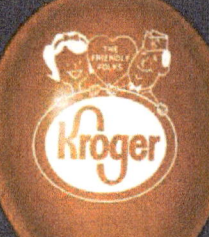

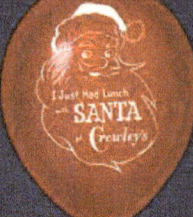

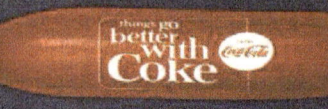

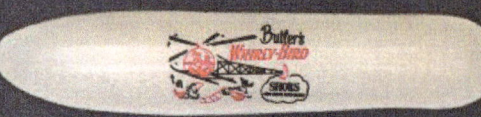

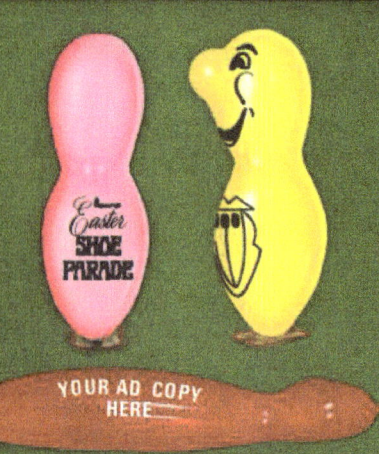

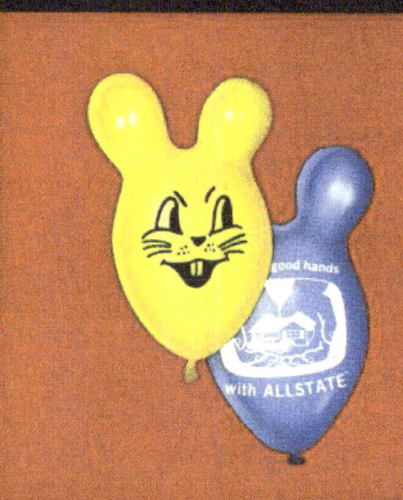

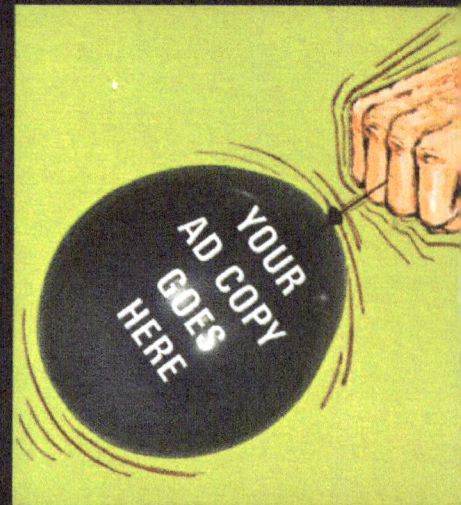

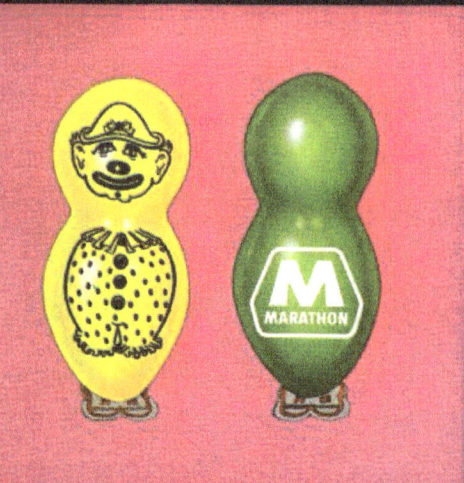

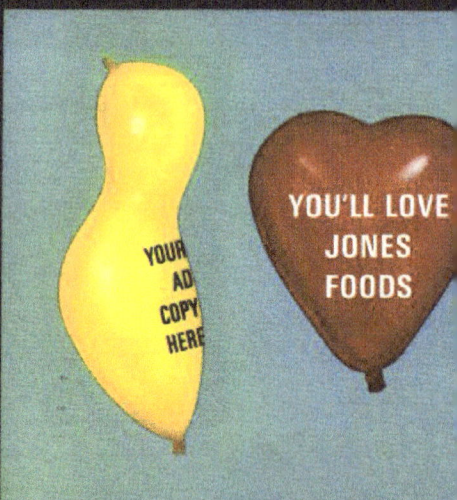

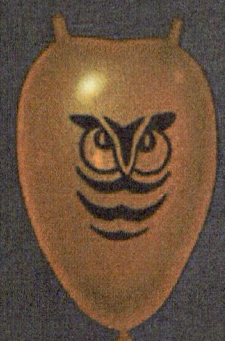

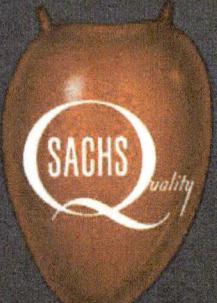

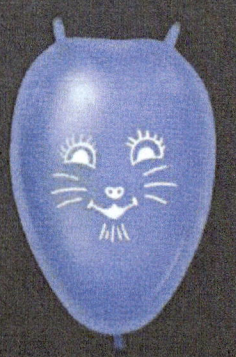

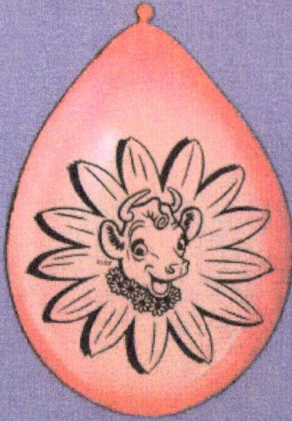

Introduction

THE IMPORTANCE OF BALLOONS

What is it about a helium-filled spherical-shaped piece of latex gently floating aloft that brings so much unbridled joy to so many souls of all ages? Whether a four year old at their first birthday party, a twenty-something at a rock concert or a retiree at an extravagant ball, the sheer sight of a balloon brings an inexplicable smile to ones face and delight to their heart.

Almost every person, big or small, young or old, has fond memories involving balloons. In the mid-2000s, I had the good fortune of seeing alternative rock band, The Flaming Lips, play at Blossom Music Center in Cuyahoga Falls. The highlight of the night, at least for this humble scribe, was a balloon drop and the subsequent frivolity as we audience members joyfully batted about the balloons.

Is it the shapes and colors or their simplicity that bring us joy? Balloons are a sort of blank slate that allow children to imagine and adults to reminisce about their childhood. Perhaps, in some small way, we find the ability to live vicariously through them and project our desire to float on the air and defy gravity: to escape our fast-paced, rat race and drift off on a breeze as the sun shines down on us.

There is no shortage of films, nightly news stories, and documentaries about balloons. Disney's film *Up* depicts an elderly gentleman who uses hundreds of balloons to carry his home away. Balloon boy, while a hoax, was an international news story about a young boy that was thought to have been carried away in a homemade flying saucer. And who can forget the countless daredevils who risk their lives by tying balloons to lawnchairs as a means of escape. The stories are nearly as plentiful as the balloons they involve. Next time you see a balloon being blown up, played with, or floating into the sky, try not to smile, thinking about happier times and some bygone moment in your past. It may be more difficult than you think.

MAPLE CITY RUBBER COMPANY

Balloons are always a crowd pleaser when employed at a vast variety of events, including concerts, balls, and parades. Pictured, is a Fourth of July parade float, created by Maple City Rubber employees and relatives, moving slowly through downtown Norwalk, decorated with Tuf-Tex balloons in a design brimming with patriotism and pride in our shared American heritage.

Above: A sight that would delight a toddler and an old timer alike: hundreds of balloons soaring weightlessly through the summer sky. Photo credit: Photo by Natasha D'Souza, via Flickr Creative Commons.

Facing page: "Who uses balloons?" The resounding answer, as stated in this advertisement, is everybody. Balloons can be used for virtually any event, be it a private or commercial affair. They are the perfect accessory for birthday parties, anniversaries, conventions, and just about any other occasion.

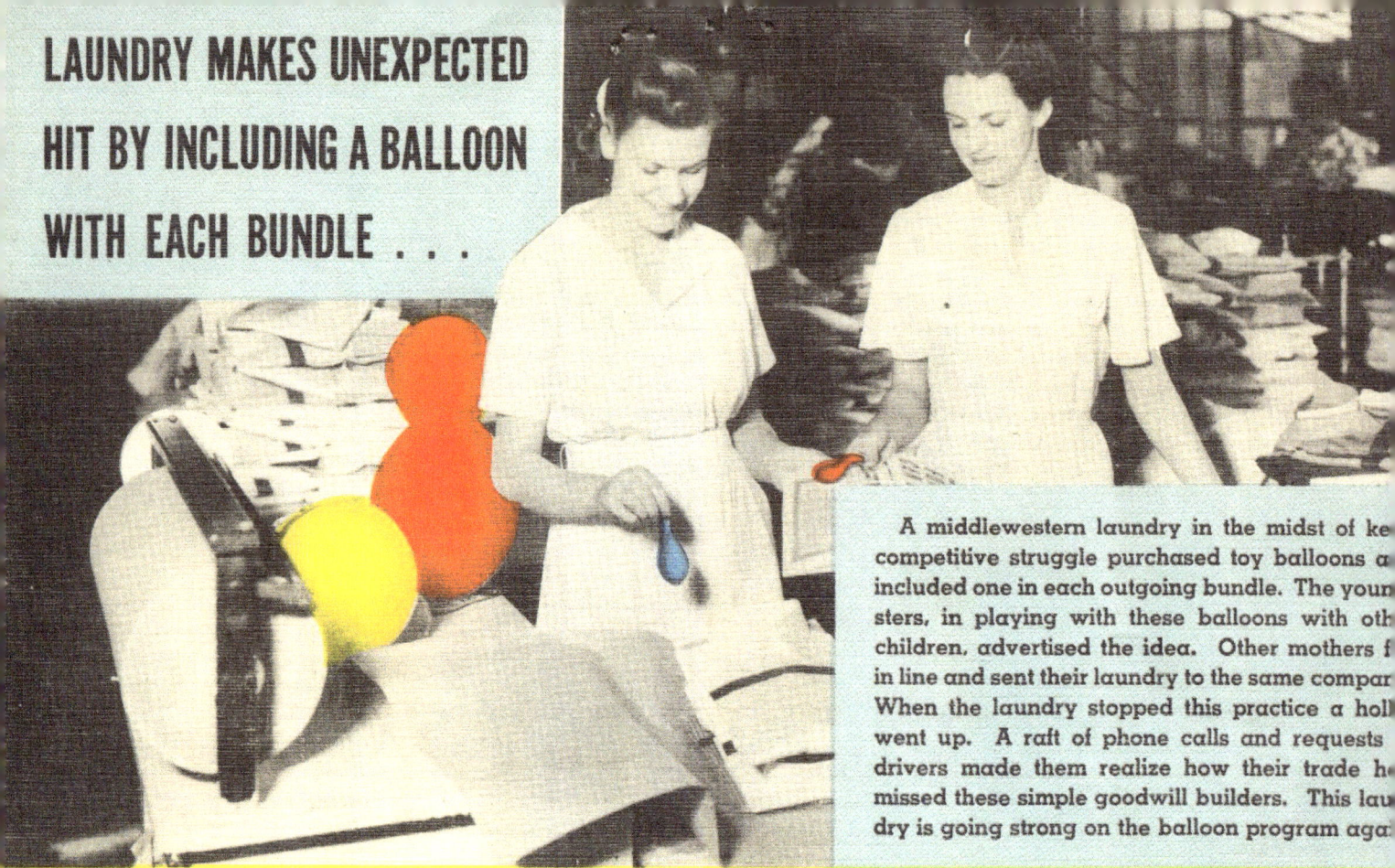

LAUNDRY MAKES UNEXPECTED HIT BY INCLUDING A BALLOON WITH EACH BUNDLE . . .

A middlewestern laundry in the midst of ke[en] competitive struggle purchased toy balloons a[nd] included one in each outgoing bundle. The youn[g]sters, in playing with these balloons with oth[er] children, advertised the idea. Other mothers f[ell] in line and sent their laundry to the same compar[y]. When the laundry stopped this practice a holl[er] went up. A raft of phone calls and requests [to] drivers made them realize how their trade h[ad] missed these simple goodwill builders. This lau[n]dry is going strong on the balloon program aga[in].

THE CHILDREN KNOW WHY THEY LIKE TO BUY AT THIS DRUG STOR[E]

This kindly druggist takes a minute or two off [to] give balloons to the youngsters who come in wi[th] their parents. This may seem trivial procedu[re] to the hard-boiled business man. Indeed it is n[ot]. When parents mention going to a drug store, t[he] youngsters are quick to lead them to the druggi[st] with the balloons. In fact, he reports that the litt[le] tots often come trying to buy bread in his dru[g] store. Such is the pulling power of balloons. [It] is wise procedure to cultivate young oncomi[ng] customers.

100 YEARS AND GROWING

Balloon Party Is Great Fun

Children playing with balloon as ball

By LILIAN CAMPBELL

WHY NOT give a balloon party for the children or the grownups during the holiday season? Everyone loves gaily colored balloons. It is fun to blow them up, and you can have a contest to see who blows his up first and biggest.

Table tennis is one game that can be played with balloons. As it is illustrated here, a tape is stretched across a table approximately 12 inches above the table surface. A player stands at each end of the table, and, with his open hand, hits a 10-inch balloon over the string to the opposing player. When struck by the server, the balloon must clear the tape and touch the table before it can be returned by the opponent. Should either player fail to hit the balloon over the tape, or should either bat the balloon off the table, the opponent scores a point. The player scoring 21 points first wins.

Facing page: A midwestern laundry has unprecedented success after launching a shrewd campaign to include a balloon with each outgoing bundle of laundry. Meanwhile, a druggist drums up business simply by taking the time to blow up balloons for pint-sized patrons. Balloons provide simple pleasure (and profit) wherever they are present.

No. 662,618. Patented Nov. 27, 1900.
H. B. CAMP.
COUPLING FOR STONEWARE PIPES.
(Application filed Sept. 6, 1900.)
(No Model.)

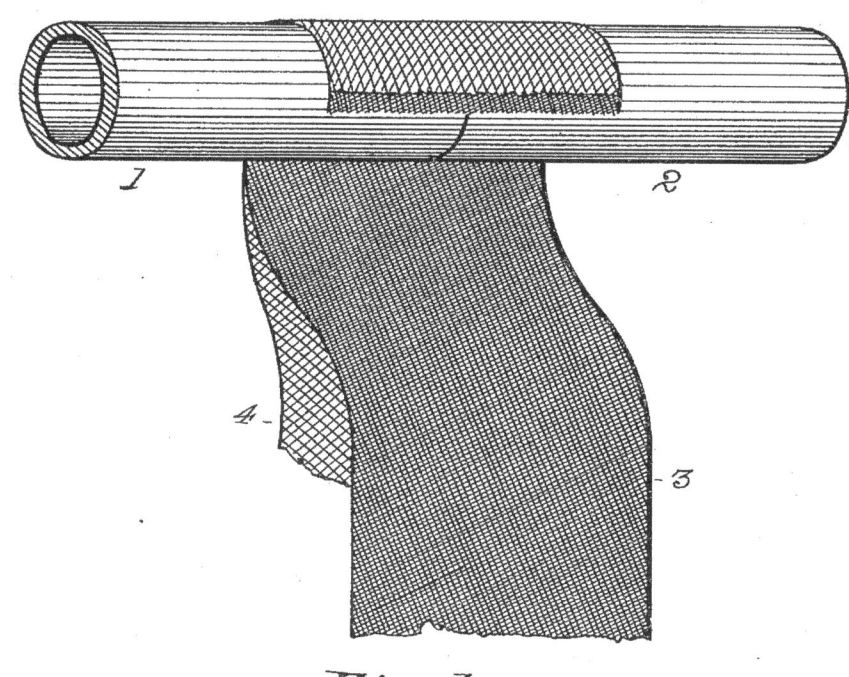

Fig. 1.

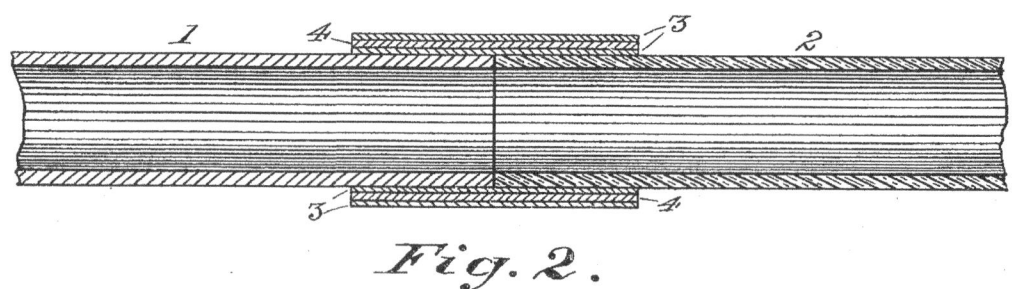

Fig. 2.

Witnesses:
Anna S Lee
Bessie Crook

Inventor:
Horace B. Camp,
By Humphrey & Humphrey,
Attorneys.

Founders

1

Our story begins during the fall of 1884, as Joseph and Julia Martin welcomed their only son into the world, Claud Victor Martin. His early years unfolded thirty miles south of Norwalk amid the rolling hills and farms of Ashland, Ohio. It was here that young Mr. Martin would first come into contact with rubber manufacturing and set him on a trajectory that would eventually lead to the formation of the Red Cross Rubber Company, original name of the Maple City Rubber Company.

As a young man in his twenties, Claud witnessed the arrival of the Camp Rubber Co. to Ashland, Ohio in 1903. The company's founder, Horace B. Camp, was a jack-of-all-trades, dabbling in the management and formation of numerous organizations in addition to dozens of patents he possessed. Among these were patents for everything from fence posts and improved methods in the construction of subway to couplings for stoneware pipes as illustrated on the previous page.

Northeast Ohio was already a focal point of rubber manufacturing prior to the opening of Camp Rubber. By the turn of the century, Akron was host to Goodrich in 1870, Goodyear which opened its doors in 1898, and Firestone following shortly thereafter in 1900.

The company was named after its president, founder, and prolific inventor, Horace B. Camp. Land was purchased and construction began a year prior with $50,000 and a bonus provided by the city of Ashland. Having relocated operations from Akron, Camp would merge his company with the West Virginia based Faultless Rubber Company in 1907. With the

Facing page: An illustration from Horace B. Camp's patent explaining how to couple stoneware pipes. "Having thus described my invention, What I claim, and desire to secure by Letters Patent, is an improved pipe-coupling consisting of a strip of fabric saturated with asphaltum wrapped about the adjacent ends of the pipe sections in combination with a metallic band having interstices to permit the asphaltum to unite the layers of fabric and wrapped in alternate layers with the fabric about the pipe ends substantially as shown and described." Photo credit: U.S. Patent and Trademark Office.

MAPLE CITY RUBBER COMPANY

The Faultless brand trademark. Photo credit: U.S. Patent and Trademark Office.

An array of rubber goods began pouring out of Northeast Ohio in the late nineteenth century. Here, the big three tire manufacturers which called Akron home can be seen together. Photo credit: Curt Teich & Co.

This page from the 1910 Federal Census shows a young Claud V. Martin as a foreman at the [Faultless] rubber works, the earliest employer to ply him with such experience.

merger and subsequent expansion, hundreds of workers from Ashland and its environs found gainful employment, including the ambitious Mr. Martin. The 1910 Federal Census lists a 27 year old Claud as foreman at the rubber works: invaluable experience for a man who would soon go on to oversee the formation and operation of his own company.

Claud had been with Faultless only a year, having joined the company just two years after reconfiguration. A brief article on Faultless Rubber states that, "The goods manufactured by this company are in general use in every country on the globe where rubber goods are in demand and wherever they are sold their products are recognized as being of the highest standard

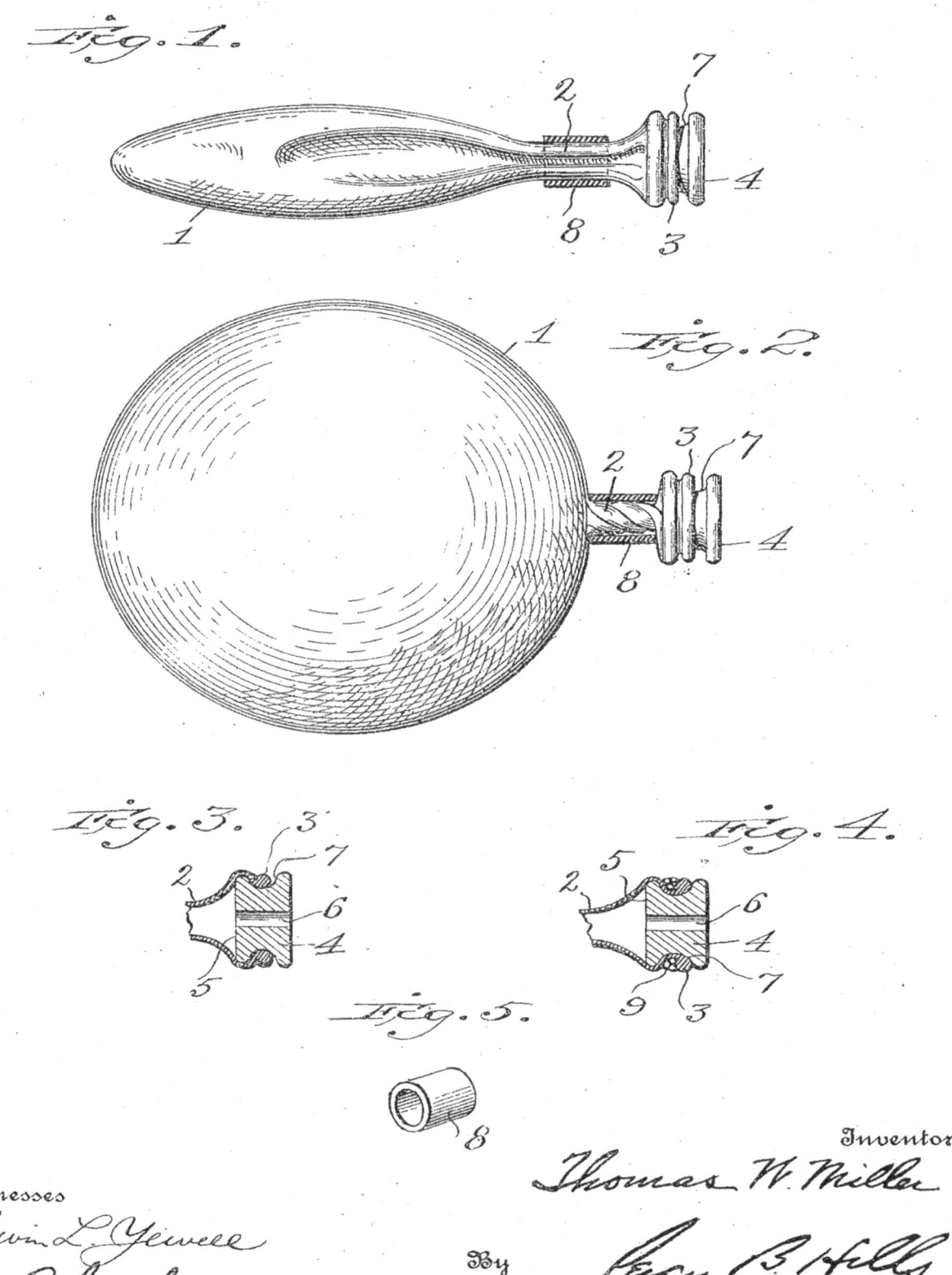

With its exaggerated dimensions, this stylized rendering of the Faultless Rubber Factory captures the expansive nature of its plant in Ashland, Ohio. Photo credit: Ashland Ohio Chapter of the Ohio Genealogical Society.

Facing page: Among the many patents registered by the Faultless Rubber Company, was this document depicting a mechanism to keep air in an inflated balloon. "My invention relates to toy balloons and similar inflatable articles, and has found object to provide the article with an improved means for retaining thereon the inflating medium, which readily may be manipulated either to close or to open the same. In the accompanying drawing figure 1 is a side elevation of a toy balloon in collapsed or uninflated condition and embodying my improved device. The operating figure 2 is a similar view, showing the balloon inflated and the parts adjusted to retain the inflating medium therein. Fig. 3 is a detail sectional view of the balloon neck and the apertured mouth-piece inserted therein. Fig. 4 is a view similar to Fig. 3 showing .a slightly modified construction. Fig. 5 is a detail perspective view of the operating collar. 1" Photo credit: U.S. Patent and Trademark Office.

MARRIAGE RECORD.

222

No. 14161.

Probate Court, Ashland County, Ohio.

MARRIAGE LICENSE. APPLICATION.

In the matter of Charles Henry Switzer and Daisy Lucile Martin

To the Honorable Judge of the Probate Court of said County:

The undersigned respectfully makes application for a Marriage License for said parties, and upon oath states:

That said Charles Henry Switzer is 35 years of age on the 13" day of July 1911, his residence is Ashland, Ohio, his place of birth is Iowa, his occupation is Clerk, his father's name is John Switzer, his mother's maiden name was Menerva Bickett, that he was ___ previously married and that he has no wife living.

That said Daisy Lucile Martin is 35 years of age on the 21" day of Sept. 1911, her residence is Ashland, Ashland County, O., her place of birth is " " " ", her occupation is Clerk, her father's name is Joseph Martin, her mother's maiden name was Julia Heygood, that she was not previously married and is not a widow or divorced woman, her married name being ___, that she has no husband living.

That neither of said parties is an habitual drunkard, epileptic, imbecile or insane, and is not under the influence of any intoxicating liquor or narcotic drug.

Said parties are not nearer of kin than second cousins, and there is no legal impediment to their marriage.

It is expected that Rev. Bowers is to solemnize the marriage of said parties.

Sworn to before me and signed in my presence, this 8" day of Nov. 1911.

C H Switzer

S. Y. McAdoo, Probate Judge.

By Gertie Mercer, Deputy Clerk.

Consent: ___

ENTRY.

Probate Court, Ashland County, Ohio, Nov 8" 1911.

Marriage License was this day granted to Charles Henry Switzer and Miss Daisy Lucile Martin.

S. Y. McAdoo, PROBATE JUDGE.

MARRIAGE CERTIFICATE. No. 14161.

The State of Ohio, Ashland County, ss.

I do hereby certify, that on the 8th day of November A. D. 1911, I solemnized the Marriage of Mr. Charles Henry Switzer with Miss Daisy Lucile Martin

Rev Albert Bowers
Congregational) Ashland

Filed and Recorded Nov 9th 1911

S. Y. McAdoo, PROBATE JUDGE.

Rev welty D.C.

of quality possible." The line of products manufactured by Faultless Rubber included everything from balloons and dolls, to rubber gloves, although their focus would eventually shift solely to medical and hygiene supplies.

It was during his tenure with Faultless Rubber that Mr. Martin would first meet his future business partner and brother-in-law, Charles H. Switzer. Born and raised in Iowa, Charles' family had roots in the Buckeye state: his parents made the long journey west before the birth of their son. Having grown and started a family of his own, Charles would eventually move his parents back to Ashland, Ohio following the passing of his first wife Mildred at 27.

A farmer by trade in Iowa, Charles took work amidst Ashland's factories, finding employment initially in a local lumber mill before finding a position with Faultless Rubber. He would soon meet Daisy Lucile Martin, Claud's older sister, and their marriage would be the catalyst that would lead to his eventual partnership with Claud Martin and the formation of Maple City Rubber four years later.

Facing page: The Ashland County marriage record of Charles H. Switzer and Daisy L. Martin, uniting the families of the two founders of Red Cross Rubber.

The Maple City Rubber Company headquarters/factory, once known as the Red Cross Rubber, as it appeared at the onset of the company in 1915. The headquarters/factory have always resided at that exact location—55 Newton St. in Norwalk, OH.

The interior of the mortgage deed for the Maple City Rubber Company headquarters/factory with the signatures of the company founders Claud Martin Sr. and Charles Switzer, as well as their beloved wives, Grace and Daisy (respectively).

Origins

2

After an eight year stint with Faultless Rubber Company, Claud V. Martin Sr. teamed up with his brother-in-law, Charles Switzer, to establish the Red Cross Rubber Company. The year was 1915 and initially the focus was on rubber novelty products, mainly toy balloons as opposed to the later migration to advertising balloons. They scoured the area for the perfect location to build a factory but opted instead to retrofit an old rooming house located at 55 Newton St. in Norwalk, Ohio. The factory still stands in the same location 100 years later, albeit with numerous cosmetic alterations and additions.

There was much industry in the region in the early twentieth century as various factories peppered Norwalk and the surrounding area. The balloon market was competitive, especially with their bitter competitor, the Oak Rubber Company. The rival company, based out of Ravenna, OH, was a major distributor of "bubbles of joy" (their name for balloons). For a while, Oak Rubber Company was the largest balloon manufacturer in the world, but like almost all of Red Cross Rubber's competition, they too would eventually fold. Initially, Red Cross Rubber Company manufactured a variety of "light rubber goods." Hot water bottles, gloves, and mats were just some of the products they manufactured, before production focused primarily on toy balloons.

It was during these early years of product exploration and innovation that Red Cross Rubber went by a name now synonymous with another organization, the American Red Cross. Originating in 1881 rather inauspiciously, the Red Cross began with a smattering of volunteers providing help and relief to victims of natural disasters, war and other catastrophes and hardships. During World War I, the American Red Cross started to grow exponentially. Their notoriety and reputation was immense due to their large scale humanitarian efforts during the war; therefore they could not afford to be confused with any other organizations. A mutual agreement came about in 1917

MAPLE CITY RUBBER COMPANY

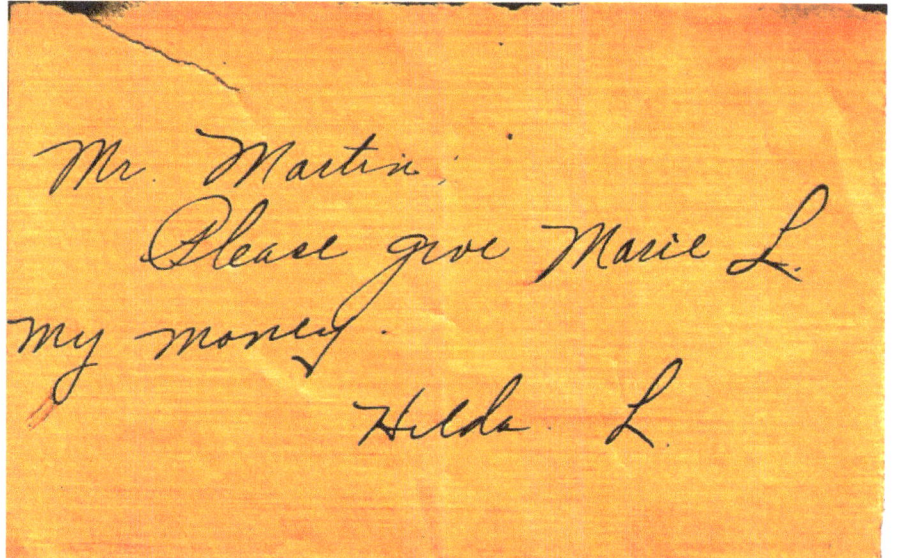

The inside of the 1920 bonus envelope illustrates the generosity of a Maple City Rubber Company employee and the bond that connects everyone who works for the company, as a selfless employee offers her bonus to another (probably) less fortunate co-worker.

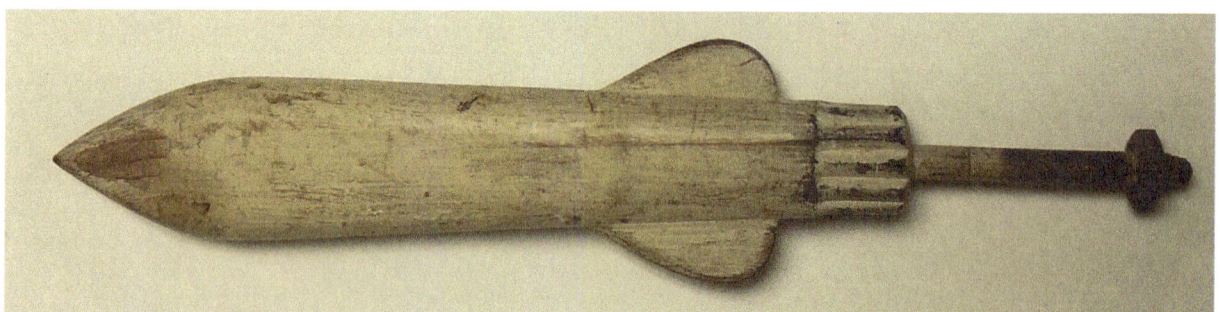

One of the earliest balloon form prototypes was this wooden rocket ship design. It never made it off the ground and is regulated to the outskirts of Maple City Rubber history.

From the moment of their inception through the present day, Maple City Rubber Company has been known for providing their employees with extremely generous bonuses. Ken Spaar said of the bonuses: "We treated em good. They always got a nice Christmas bonus." This is a year-end bonus envelope dated 1920.

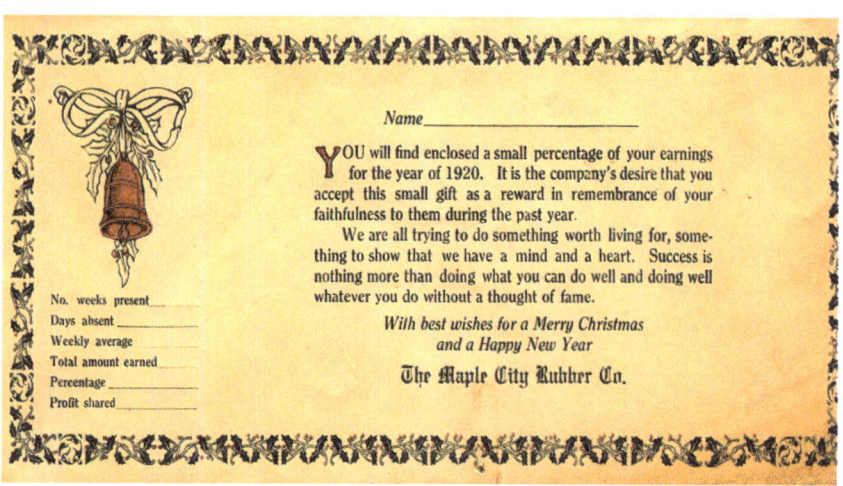

between the humanitarian organization and the upstart balloon company for the latter to change its moniker; thus Red Cross Rubber became Maple City Rubber Company.

Maple City Rubber Company filed as a for-profit corporation on December 17, 1917. In a short time, Maple City Rubber Company grew quite successful. Sales were soaring not only in the states, but also abroad, as evidenced by a local newspaper article touting an "enormous shipment of toy balloons" being sent by the company to merry old England.

The profits were not only reaped for the owners, but also the employees. Martin and Switzer were renowned for sharing their windfall with the staff, particularly in the form of an extremely generous year-end bonus.

A few years passed and operations and production within Maple City Rubber hummed with efficiency. But things would take a tragic turn on March 8, 1920. While standing on the factory floor, Charles Switzer was impaled by a runaway rod that had been jarred loose from one of the compressors, hurling itself at a high velocity right through his solar plexus. With the tragic and gruesome death of Mr. Switzer the company was briefly commandeered by the elder Martin. Switzer's half of the company was willed to his son and heir Millard, but at the time he was a mere twelve years of age and far too young to shoulder the vast responsibility that comes with presiding over a major manufacturer of latex balloons.

Upon completion of his studies, Millard joined The Maple City Rubber Company in September 1927. He remained with the company for more than 60 years where he worked closely with both Claud Sr. and Claude Jr. in managing the sales efforts, setting direction and guiding the company through unparalleled growth.

It seemed like profits would steadily increase and the company would continue to grow, but then the stock market crashed in 1929, bringing a temporary end to a great American success story. The Great Depression brought with it many a hardship for Maple City Rubber Company, but as always it persevered. While many other companies in the region had to shut down, Maple City Rubber Company was able to weather the storm due to its dedicated staff and superior line of products.

MAPLE CITY RUBBER COMPANY

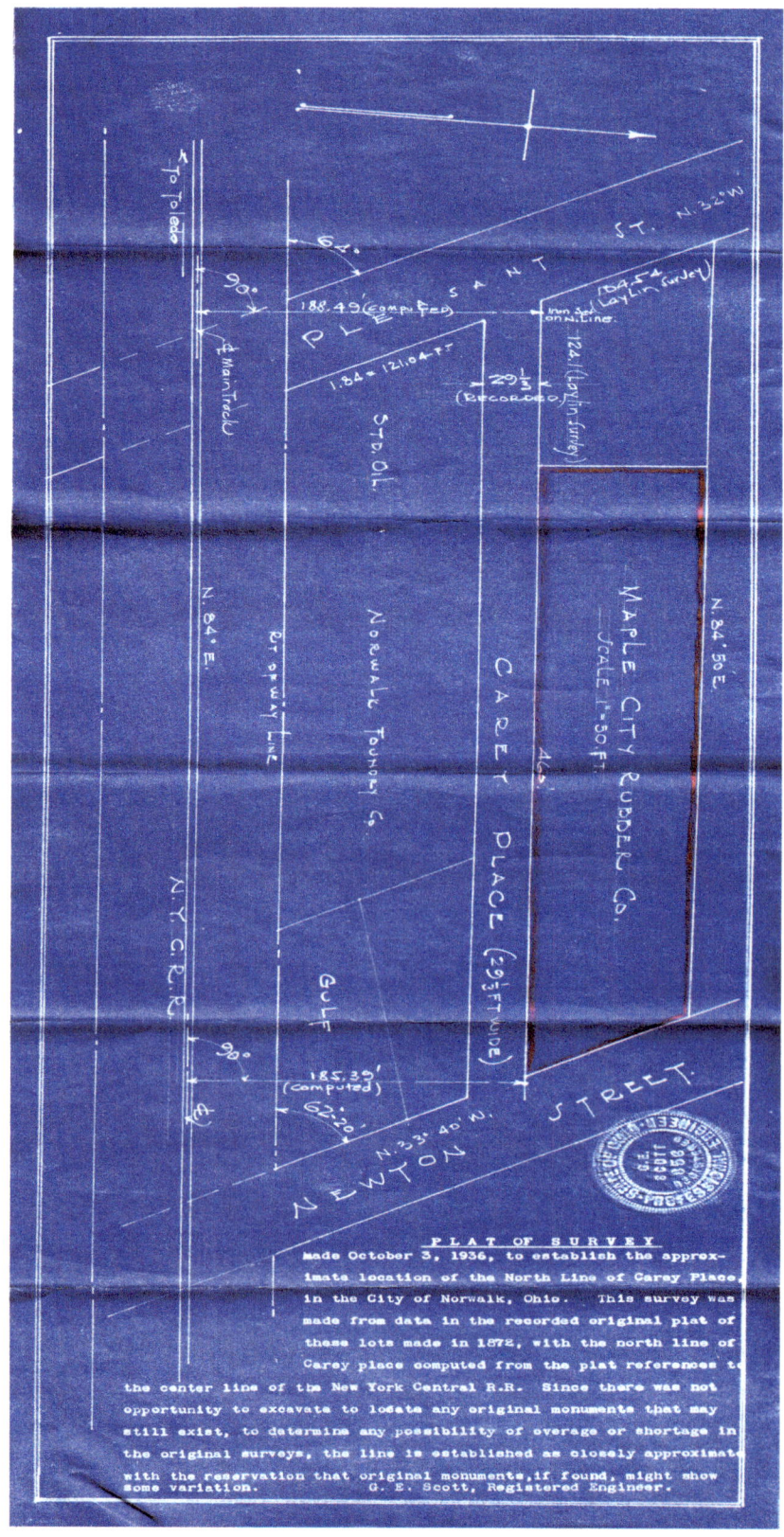

Plat of land survey conducted on October 3, 1936 to determine "the approximate location of the north line of Carey Place in the city of Norwalk, Ohio." Carey Place is a tiny street that runs between Newton Street and Pleasant Street. Maple City Rubber Company is prominently displayed at the top of the plat.

Cover of the mortgage deed for Maple City Rubber Company headquarters/factory. The deed was received on January 15, 1917 and recorded eight days later. In essence, the founders of the company (Claud V. Martin and Charles Switzer) were selling the deed to themselves for $1.

During the War

3

The long term impact of the Great Depression continued to shape the world for years. Maple City Rubber managed to weather the economic hardship when many other factories simply could not. Procedures and practices, however, would not return to normal as war and conflict were on the horizon. Hostilities in the Far East, home to much of the world's natural rubber production, led to a shortage of the material and an increased need for synthetic rubber. A majority of crude rubber, at this time, came from British Malaya and the Dutch East Indies. The Sandusky Register reported that "by the late 1930s, the United States was using half the world's supply of natural rubber." Following a few setbacks, reliance on synthetic rubber, like DuPont's neoprene, was on the rise by many manufacturers including Maple City Rubber during WWII. Sources state that "as Japan moved to conquer Southeast Asia, 90% of the world's natural rubber suddenly became unavailable to the United States."

At the onset of World War II, Maple City Rubber introduce the industry standard line of durable Tuf-Tex balloons only to have production suspended shortly thereafter. In 1940, Franklin Roosevelt, calling rubber a "strategic and critical material," created the Rubber Reserve Company (RRC), to stockpile natural rubber and regulate synthetic rubber production. Various sources state Firestone, B.F. Goodrich, Goodyear, and U.S. Rubber agreed to work together to solve the nation's wartime rubber needs.

Along with paper, rags, and various metals, Americans were encouraged to do their part and aid through the conservation and donation of scrap rubber for the war. Many contributed and Maple City Rubber was no exception. A scrap metal drive and drop off point was established on factory grounds with proceeds being delivered by Claud Sr. and his wife Grace to the Huron County Service Club. But Maple City Rubber's real contribution to the war effort came via the production of football bladders, gun gussets, and other important rubber items per contract with the U.S. government.

Facing page: Boys and girls are seen selling various pieces of scrap rubber at a northeast Ohio gas station and automotive repair shop. Photo credit: Cleveland Press Collection, Clevland State University.

The Maple City Rubber Company

Manufacturers of

RUBBER NOVELTIES AND DRUG SUNDRIES

NORWALK, OHIO,

Gentlemen:

Due to the present shortage of crude rubber and other material, and because of the action taken by Priorities Division, War Industries Board, Washington, D. C., we have filed with the Priorities Division War Industry Board a pledge signed by the President and Treasurer of our company. As this pledge was same as ones enclosed, we are obliged to ask you to return one of the enclosed pledges properly signed--retaining one for your own file. We request that you give this matter your prompt attention as we will not be permitted to deliver any of our products until one of the enclosed pledges has been properly signed and returned to us.

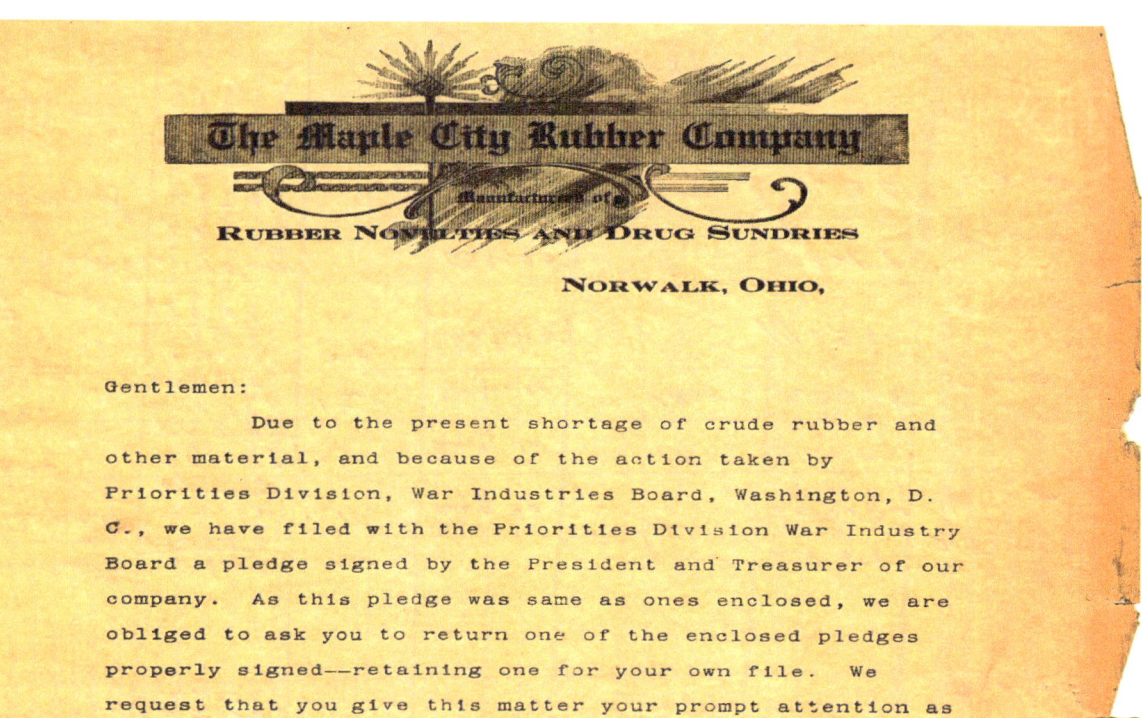

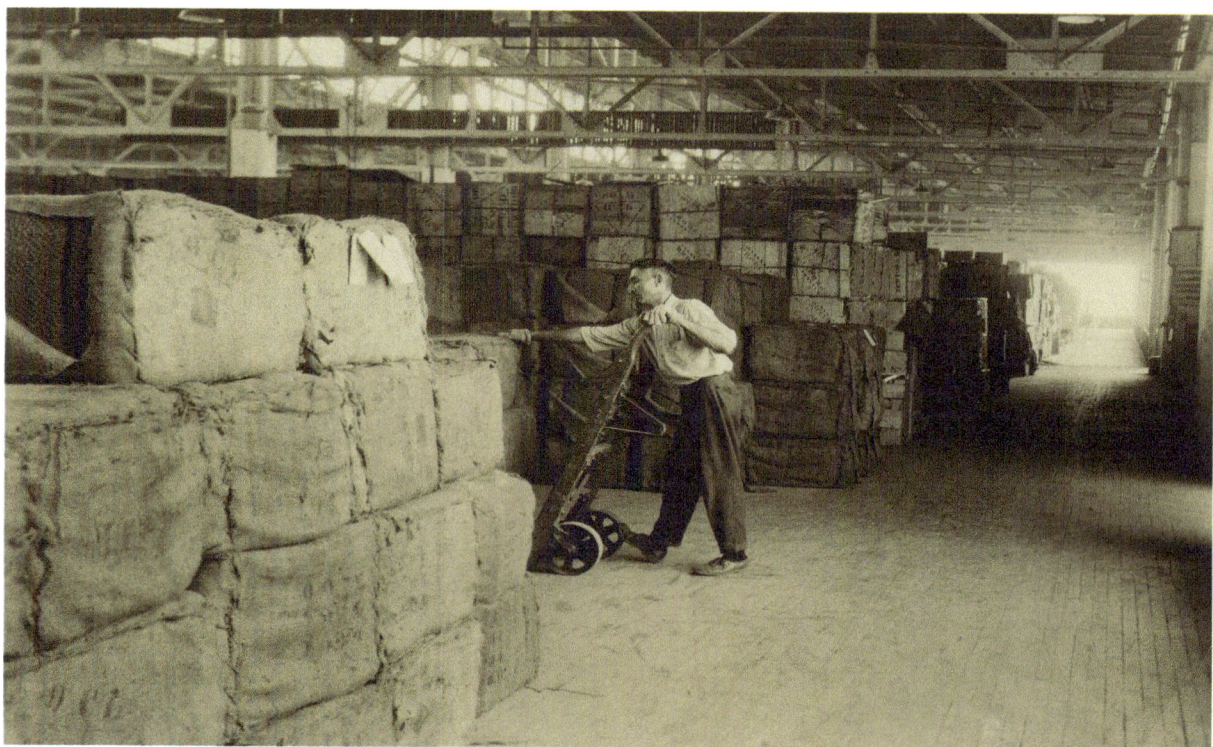

Lower Image: An image depicting a loading dock stacked high with crude rubber bales. Photo credit: Cleveland Press Collection, Cleveland State University.

Facing Page: To bolster civilian participation in the war effort, signs and posters like these were created and displayed for all to see. Photo credit: U.S. Government.

A Gas Mask requires 1.11 pounds of rubber

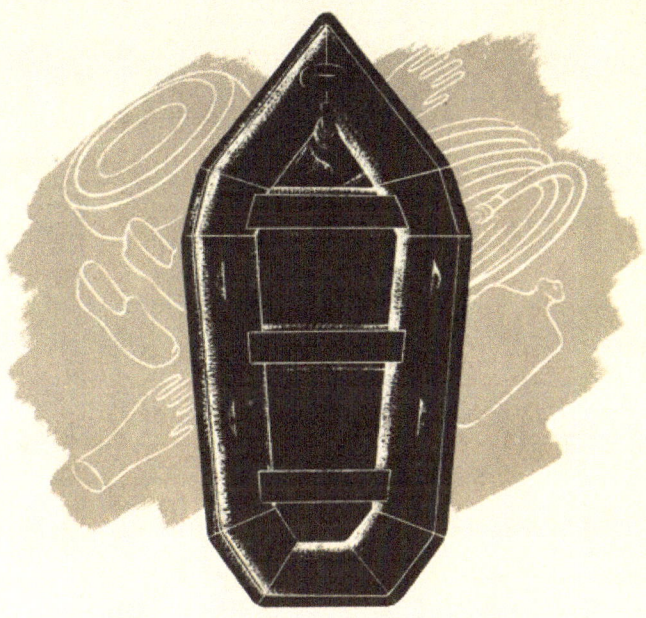

A Life Raft requires 17 to 100 pounds of rubber

A Scout Car requires 306 pounds of rubber

A Heavy Bomber requires 1,825 pounds of rubber

America needs your SCRAP RUBBER

WAR PRODUCTION BOARD
Bureau of Industrial Conservation

100 YEARS AND GROWING

A postcard illustrating an aerial view of one of DuPont's many plants. A scientist by the name of Dr. Elmer Bolton discovered neoprene in early 1930.

Football, as well as other pastimes, were meant to distract and boost morale during the War, aiding civilians and soldiers alike in coping with the horrors of combat. The Federal Government contracted with Maple City Rubber to manufacture football bladders. Here, "A new use for the versatile jeep, as it's being substituted for a charging sled. This photo was taken in November 1943 at Camp Joseph T. Robinson in Arkansas. Capt. C. R. Goodwin, Special Projects Officer of the 66th Division at the camp, is getting a "ride" while directing the training of a gridiron team which is part of the camp's athletic program in November 1943." Photo credit: U.S. Army.

Facing page: Photo credit: U.S. National Archives and Records Administration.

ANOTHER TUF-TEX *first!*

WHIRLYBIRD

PENNY BALLOON

The Hottest and Fastest Selling Penny Balloon Ever Offered!
Packed 2 Gross to a Box
28 Gross to a Case - Wt. 13 lbs.   56 Gross to a Case - Wt. 26 lbs.
Full Assortment of Seven Colors - Price - $1.60 per bx.
Terms 2-10-30 FOB Factory - Freight Paid on 100# or Over

THE MAPLE CITY RUBBER COMPANY
NORWALK, OHIO

USE THIS HANDY ORDER FORM FOR PROMPT SHIPMENT

THE MAPLE CITY RUBBER CO.
Norwalk, Ohio

Please ship _____ boxes Whirlybird Penny Balloons at $1.60 per box.
☐ Send information and prices on complete line.

NAME _____

STREET _____

CITY _____   STATE _____

BY _____

The Post War Years

4

With the War's end, Maple City Rubber Company resumed production of its line of balloons and life slowly returned to normal. The Tuf-Tex line of balloons, which began in 1940, was alive and well. Once again, the balloons produced were being shipped and supplied to distributors around the world. New shapes and designs were being produced to the delight of children everywhere. Where celebrations and festivities were being held, Maple City Rubber balloons were present. Locally, they sponsored Independence Day festivities and fireworks for the community to enjoy as well as parades. To many involved and employed with the company, the community has always been viewed as something of an extension of the familial atmosphere felt within the workplace. Most residents of Norwalk and its environs had worked or knew someone who had worked for Maple City Rubber Company.

By the 1950s, Maple City Rubber was cited in the *Norwalk Reflector-Herald* as the "oldest manufacturing establishment in the city in point of continuous operation under the same management." Claud Martin Sr. had been at the helm for nearly forty years. In 1959, Martin Sr. was recognized by the local chapter of the Jaycees for his service and generosity in helping groom young individuals personally and professionally for the workplace.

Never one to slow down, Martin Sr. continued to work into his fifth decade with the company. To mark the occasion, expansive new facilities were constructed. The *Norwalk Reflector-Herald* reported, "A two story addition of 32,000 square feet is being built at the Maple City Rubber Company plant, 55 Newton St. Claud V. Martin Sr., presi-

Facing page: An order form for one of the many balloons produced and distributed by Maple City Rubber. The Whirlybird was less about the imagination and more about the frantic, excited spinning it produced as air escaped.

dent, said the added area will be used for both manufacturing and warehousing and that the number of employees at the plant may be increased when the space is put into use. Work on the addition was started last week by Jennings and Churella Construction Co. of New London. It is expected to be completed by mid-July. The building permit application indicates construction costs are estimated at $35,000."

Tragedy, however, struck midday on Thursday, September 8th, 1966 when the 80 year old Mr. Martin Sr. fell down a flight of stairs while at a local eatery. He died the next day from his injuries, leaving behind his wife of 55 years, Grace, and the company he had put considerable effort into. The end of an era had come. What started as an idea shared between two men a half century earlier, had grown into a leader in balloon production. It was time for a new generation to take up the reins.

Shiny new equipment populates the recently constructed wing of Maple City Rubber, adding much needed space and upgrades to the production line.

100 YEARS AND GROWING

Not an unhappy face among the bunch, Maple City Rubber employees can be seen here taking a break from work and playing cards together.

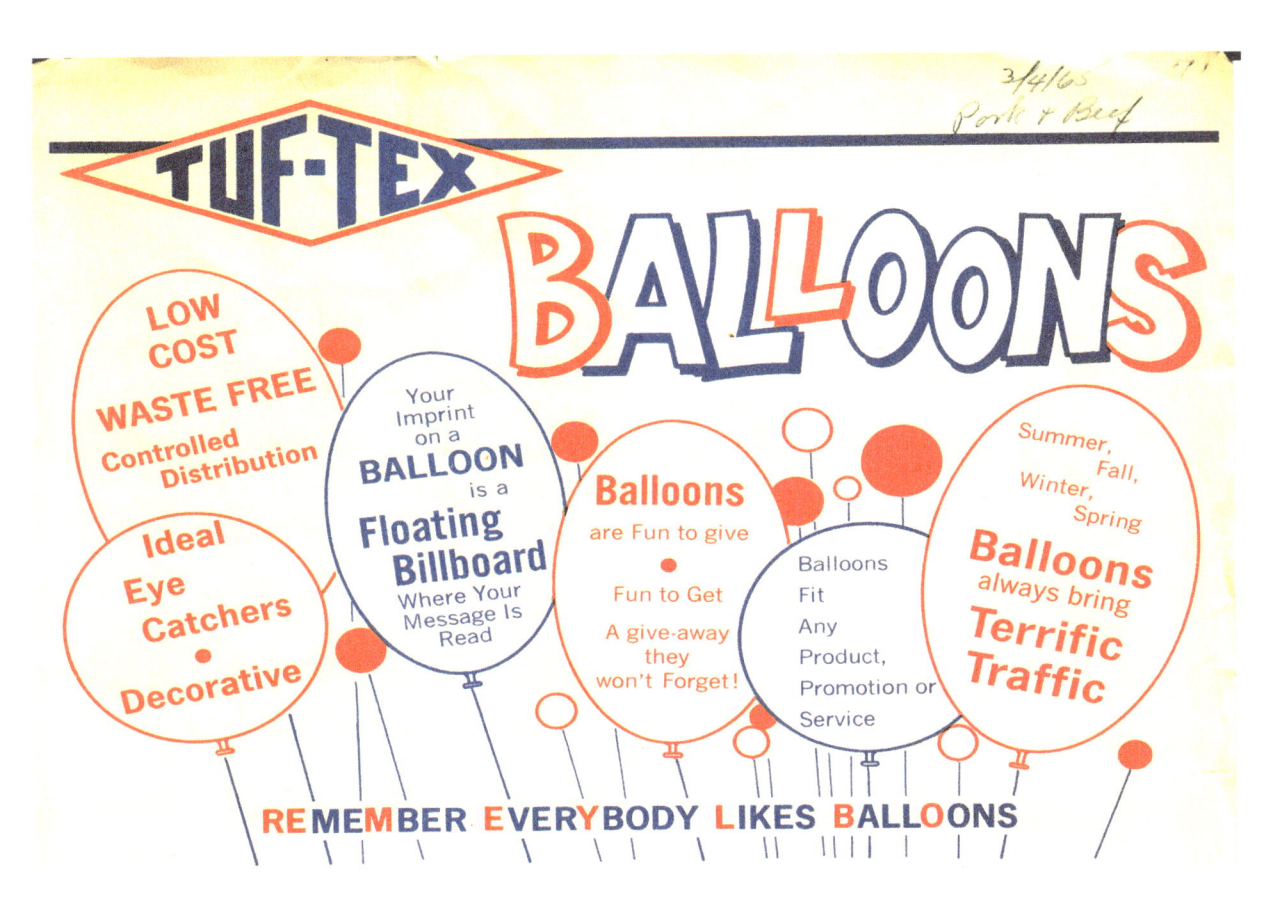

TUF-TEX BALLOONS

- LOW COST
- WASTE FREE
- Controlled Distribution
- Ideal Eye Catchers
- Decorative

Your Imprint on a BALLOON is a **Floating Billboard** Where Your Message Is Read

Balloons are Fun to give • Fun to Get • A give-away they won't Forget!

Balloons Fit Any Product, Promotion or Service

Summer, Fall, Winter, Spring **Balloons** always bring **Terrific Traffic**

REMEMBER EVERYBODY LIKES BALLOONS

MAPLE CITY RUBBER COMPANY

Father and son, Claud Martin Sr. on the left and Claude Jr. on the right, worked side-by-side at Maple City Rubber for two decades.

An undated image of Maple City Rubber Company staff throwing a birthday party for the senior Martin. Claud is seen blowing out the candles amidst the equipment and machinery he was so often seen walking about.

100 YEARS AND GROWING

Above, left: Small foil sticker indicating Maple City Rubber's 50th anniversary. Above, right: Simple and to the point, many small classified ads like this one ran in the local papers, aiding in the recruitment of new hires during times of growth. This was especially true following the expansion in '65-'66.

Below: Standing on your feet all day can wear you out. A small group of factory workers including Kenny Myers, Irene Fay, and Don Fey stop for refreshments and to shoot the breeze on the factory floor.

IN THE COMMON PLEAS COURT OF HURON COUNTY, OHIO

THE NATIONAL LATEX PRODUCTS COMPANY,   Case No. 35885
                    Plaintiff,
         vs.   CONSENT DECREE
MAPLE CITY RUBBER COMPANY
MILLARD B. SWITZER
CLAUDE V. MARTIN,
                    Defendants.

Whereas The National Latex Products Company, 246 E. Fourth Street, Ashland, Ohio, having filed its Petitition For Permanent Injunction, Equitable Relief, An Accounting and Damages, on April 23, 1970, the same being Case No. 35885, wherein Maple City Rubber Company, Norwalk, Ohio, and Millard B. Switzer and Claude V. Martin are named as Defendants; and

Whereas Plaintiff and Defendants desire to terminate the aforementioned action and the claims therein, do hereby consent to the entry of this final judgment without trial or adjudication of any issue of fact or law herein and without this final judgment constituting evidence or admission by any party hereto with respect to any petition:

NOW THEREFORE, before the taking of any testimony by deposition or otherwise and without trial or adjudication of any issue of fact or law herein, and upon the consent of the parties hereto, The National Latex Products Company, Maple City Rubber Company, Millard B. Switzer and Claude V. Martin, it is hereby ordered, adjudged and decreed as follows:

1. Each of the parties to said proceedings agrees that to October 14, 1978, they will not:

   i. Copy, duplicate or appropriate the design of certain automatic balloon plants manufactured by Trentham or its affiliated companies;

   ii. Disclose or furnish to anyone any information concerning the design, manufacture or use of said automatic balloon plants or permits said plants to be viewed by others for said purposes.

Page 2

2. It is further ordered, adjudged and decreed that this case is hereby dismissed with prejudice, each party to bear their own costs.   No record.

Dated _____, 1970

_____
                    Judge

We hereby approve and consent to the foregoing decree:

THE NATIONAL LATEX PRODUCTS COMPANY
246 E. Fourth Street
Ashland, Ohio
By _____
   Barry R. Gill, II, President

MAPLE CITY RUBBER COMPANY
Norwalk, Ohio
By _____
   Claude V. Martin, President

_____
Millard B. Switzer, Individually

_____
Claude V. Martin, Individually

Above: In 1970, The National Latex Company filed a lawsuit in the Common Pleas Court of Huron County, Ohio alleging that Maple City Rubber infringed upon their exclusive right to use automated machines manufactured by Trentham to produce balloons. The case was dismissed, but both companies agreed not to "copy, duplicate or appropriate the design of certain automatic balloon plants manufactured by Trentham or its affiliated companies."

Left: The switch to automated machines, such as the one pictured here, helped Maple City Rubber stay competitive with their rivals.

The Present

5

Present day Maple City Rubber Company owes much of its success and vision to the joint management of Claude Martin Jr. and Millard Switzer. Together they provided a tandem effort to deliver the very best quality product through an efficient operation (led by Claude) coupled with dynamic customer driven marketing and sales programs (created by Millard) laying a fertile base for future growth.

Maple City Rubber Company might be defunct if it weren't for a bold, if not necessarily legal, move by Claude V. Martin Jr. Soon after taking the helm of the company in the 1960s, Martin realized the company needed to evolve if it were to survive. The days of hand-dipping balloons were quickly coming to a halt; thus he acted swiftly to procure an automated machine from Trentham Manufacturing Co. Ltd. in Europe. National Latex Products, Co. based out of Ashland, OH already had purchased an automated machine from Trentham and hoped to corner the market on automated balloon manufacturing. In light of Mr. Martin's purchase National Latex Products Co. filed a million dollar lawsuit against Maple City Rubber Company claiming they had exclusive rights to operating an automated balloon plant. Of course this was unsubstantiated and the case was dismissed as it was obvious that the Ashland company was attempting to monopolize automated balloon manufacturing.

In addition to the aforementioned lawsuit, Maple City Rubber Company has withstood numerous other hardships, including the recent helium crisis of 2012. The crisis was caused, at least in part, by the government's ill-advised tactic of selling helium severely beneath the market rate, thus cultivating an atmosphere in which excessive waste was the norm. Unbelievably most of the helium used in the United States is culled

MAPLE CITY RUBBER COMPANY

Modern automated dipping machinery that replaced the old hand dipping method.

During the 1990s, Maple City Rubber Company switched from a focus on marketing their balloons for birthday parties to advertising. Car dealerships account for a large portion of their sales.

This Maple City Rubber Company ad defines helium and explains how it is the safest and most effective gas for filling balloons. It also explains how helium is solely distributed by the United States Government. In 2012, a helium crisis hit balloon manufacturers hard, including Maple City Rubber, after an initial downturn, Maple City Rubber Company is in the process of overcoming yet another major obstacle.

from a single stockpile in northern Texas; thus it is one of the few goods that is still regulated by the government. When the shortage occurred, the government only sold to the enterprises deemed most vital, namely the medical community. The impact the crisis had on the company was significant as sales plummeted and the workforce was drastically depleted.

In the 1990s, under the sure-handed direction of then president Ken Spaar, Maple City Rubber Company transitioned from producing balloons for parties to manufacturing them for advertising. Almost all other balloon manufacturers in the United States and abroad produce lower-end balloons that are best suited as toys or for birthday parties. Mr. Spaar saw this as a way to distance the Tuf-Tex Brand from lower quality imports. This proved to be a brilliant strategic move as Maple City Rubber quickly established itself as the leader in the outdoor balloon advertising market. The big seller since the switch has been the seventeen inch balloon which lends itself to advertising.

Since 1940, Tuf-Tex balloons have widely been recognized as the highest quality product on the market, only manufactured with premium

MAPLE CITY RUBBER COMPANY

Balloon Center at the Halloween & Party Show held in Chicago. This is one of the largest annual Halloween-themed trade shows in the world.

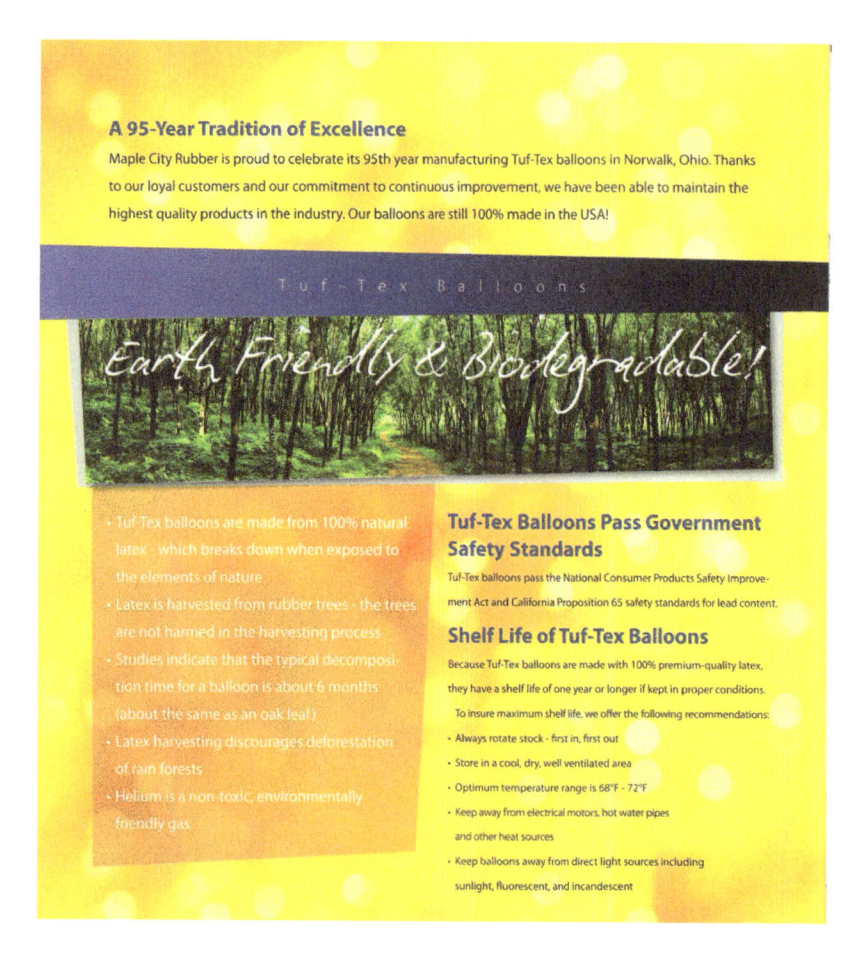

A 95-Year Tradition of Excellence

Maple City Rubber is proud to celebrate its 95th year manufacturing Tuf-Tex balloons in Norwalk, Ohio. Thanks to our loyal customers and our commitment to continuous improvement, we have been able to maintain the highest quality products in the industry. Our balloons are still 100% made in the USA!

Tuf-Tex Balloons

Earth Friendly & Biodegradable!

- Tuf-Tex balloons are made from 100% natural latex - which breaks down when exposed to the elements of nature.
- Latex is harvested from rubber trees - the trees are not harmed in the harvesting process.
- Studies indicate that the typical decomposition time for a balloon is about 6 months (about the same as an oak leaf).
- Latex harvesting discourages deforestation of rain forests.
- Helium is a non-toxic, environmentally friendly gas.

Tuf-Tex Balloons Pass Government Safety Standards

Tuf-Tex balloons pass the National Consumer Products Safety Improvement Act and California Proposition 65 safety standards for lead content.

Shelf Life of Tuf-Tex Balloons

Because Tuf-Tex balloons are made with 100% premium-quality latex, they have a shelf life of one year or longer if kept in proper conditions. To insure maximum shelf life, we offer the following recommendations:
- Always rotate stock - first in, first out
- Store in a cool, dry, well ventilated area
- Optimum temperature range is 68°F - 72°F
- Keep away from electrical motors, hot water pipes and other heat sources
- Keep balloons away from direct light sources including sunlight, fluorescent, and incandescent

Tuf-Tex balloons are the highest quality balloons on the market and more importantly, they are 100 percent environmentally safe.

100 YEARS AND GROWING

Maple City Rubber has designed balloons for a multitude of recording artists, film productions, stage shows and sporting events. This photo depicts just a smattering of the thousands of special event balloon designs Maple City Rubber Company has created, including prototypes for Elton John and Rihanna tours, the Ohio State Buckeyes and University of Michigan Wolverines football teams, and promotions for Hollywood blockbusters *Man of Steel* and *The Hobbit*.

materials. The superior quality renders a balloon high in durability, strength and vibrant color.

In 2004, Jeff Tinker (Ken's son-in-law) took the helm and worked to expand the Tuf-Tex distribution to other advertising venues such as movie sets, balloon drops, concerts, and various sporting events. Some of the biggest stars in the world have used Tuf-Tex balloons in their live shows or to promote a variety of products. Elton John, Rihanna, Britney Spears, Jack White, Motley Crue and dozens more can be counted as satisfied Tuf-Tex customers. Touring children's stage shows, such as Sesame Street and Yo Gabba Gabba have used these high quality balloons to delight youngsters across the country. If you have ever watched the Kentucky Derby or attended a Cleveland Indians or Cavs game you may have noticed promotional balloons being utilized. Those often are Tuf-Tex balloons.

MAPLE CITY RUBBER COMPANY

T'was the night before Christmas, and all through the place
Everything was a mess, an utter disgrace.
The dishes were piled- high in the sink
And the half eaten food was beginning to stink
But the wee little devils were tucked in their beds
While visions of bonuses danced in their heads
Mama in her negligee and I in the buff
Had just settled down for some sexy stuff.
When out on the lawn - there rose such a clatter
I sprang from my bed – slipped - and fell with splatter
I flew to the window and threw up the sash
I did it too hard – the pane broke with a crash
What before my wandering eyes should appear
But a bald old man – like the one standing here
His sleigh was pulled – by a large group of dames
He patted their fannies and called out their names
On Peggy – On Claudia – On Monnie – On Jo
And on down the list till there was no mo.
He jumped down the chimney and injured his foot
And stood one legged just covered with soot
The place was a mess, but who was to blame
When down the stairs - those little devils came
His glare at the mess – to the little imps went
They knew in an instant what a look like that meant
Karen and Diana made a list what to do
Barb and Marie printed it - and picked out a crew
Charlie and Bobby cleaned out the sink
And a little boy named Daniel took care of the stink (he should he made it)
Bernie and Theresa packaged the scrap
Lou and Rick hauled it out back
All the rest pitched in and soon the place shone
They washed and scrubbed it right down to the bone
He looked all around – gave a pleased little sigh
And piled up bonuses – about this high
He walked out the door – none of that chimney stuff
He tried it once and that was enough
He gave a hearty laugh – (Ho Ho Ho) ere he drove out of view
And yelled Merry Christmas to all – but especially YOU

Above left: Claude V. Martin Jr. composed (and memorized) this Christmas themed poem for the annual holiday party. He recited the poem, which mentions many employees by name, at the annual party to the delight of his workers. Above right: Just two of the many devoted Maple City Rubber employees hard at work on the factory floor, helping perfect the latest batch of American-made Tuf-Tex balloons.

Tinker remained as President thought 2013 and proved instrumental in guiding Maple City Rubber Company through the aforementioned helium crisis.

But what makes Maple City Rubber Company different? How do they stand out from other balloon companies? What separates this company most from not only other balloon companies, but most companies in general is the aforementioned sense of family felt by each and every member of the Maple City Rubber Company staff.

There is a sense of family and community that is obvious the second one sets foot on the factory floor or offices of Maple City Rubber Company. The employees, from the newest hire to the President, are treated as if they were a sibling or life-long friend. Festivities are planned for each employees birthday, featuring cake, gifts, and of course balloons. Chicanery is said to occur at a high rate, including an occasional impromptu wrestling match. But when work needs to be done the employees do so as a team with great passion and pride. The final American-made product is testament to the devotion Maple City Rubber Company employees have for their co-workers, job and company.

The sense of community, family, and togetherness extend past the factory floor. The company encourages and sponsors many extracurricular activities for the employees such as softball, volleyball and dartball teams as well as participation in community fundraising events.

There is a loyalty amongst the staff that is a rarity in the modern workforce. Very few employees leave Maple City Rubber Company, and those that do often come back within a few years of their departure. Upon being asked what he misses most about working at the company, retired President Claude V. Martin Jr. responded: "Mostly the people...we always had great people. Loyal...they were all so loyal."

It is natural for employees to develop a sense of loyalty to their employer when the employers in question are Claude Martin Jr. and Millard Switzer. In numerous interviews conducted, nary one derogatory comment was uttered regarding either of them. Perhaps their benevolence was most exemplified by one of Claude's daily routines. As president, he would walk the factory floor and personally greet every employee. They knew and cared about all of their workers.

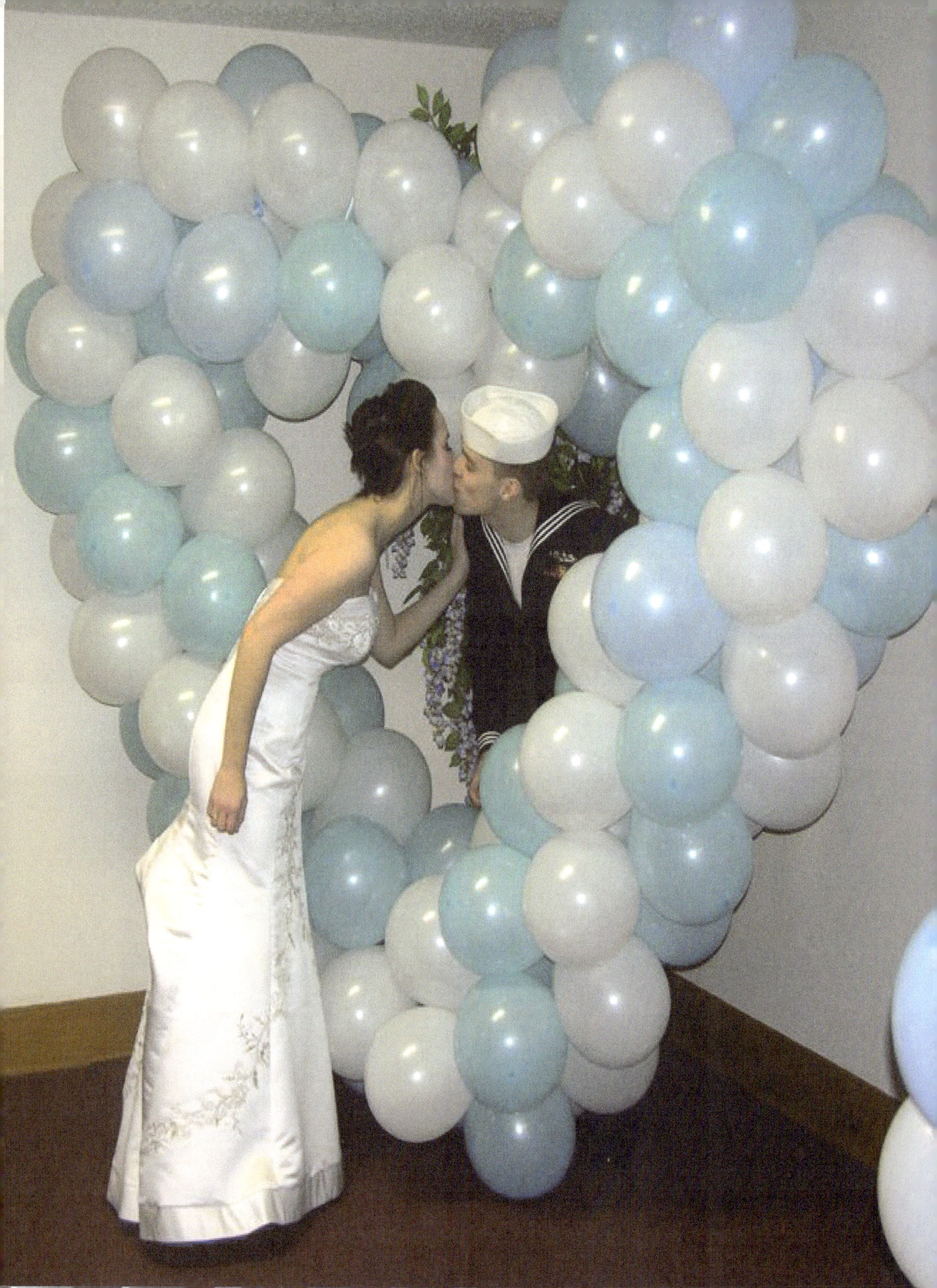

The Future

6

What does the future hold for Maple City Rubber Company? Can we expect another hundred years of sustained excellence? Maple City Rubber Company has pulled through numerous hardships including the most recent adversity caused by the global helium crisis with determination and resolve. Two world wars, a couple of economic depressions, a million dollar lawsuit, and a multitude of obstacles were no match for the company, what calamity could possibly be conjured in the next century that would lay waste to the formidable balloon manufacturer?

Maple City Rubber Company has never changed the quality of its product, from inception to present day. According to Claude V. Martin Jr.: "Maple City Rubber makes the best balloon." A high quality product, special attention to the customers, and a devoted, united workforce are the sturdy foundation which will keep Maple City Rubber Company prosperous for many years into the future. This bond is evident when you speak with any current or former employee or if you simply stride across the factory floor on a busy afternoon. Loyal, exultant employees illicit devoted customers.

Today, the leadership team of Mike Kilbane and Paul Bennett, along with all the current Maple City Rubber Compay employees are committed to perpetuating the legacy created by their predecessors. By focusing on unparalleled product quality, exemplary personalized customer service and resourceful market initiatives, they are building on the already solid foundation that will support Maple City Rubber Company for the next 100 years. After all, their work of spreading cheer is not done, there will be many more occasions to celebrate, spirits to lift and hearts to delight.

Facing page: A clever design created with Tuf-Tex balloons to help celebrate the union of two young lovebirds.

MAPLE CITY RUBBER COMPANY

The present and future of manufacturing are companies that engage in eco-friendly services and produce biodegradable products. All Tuf-Tex balloons are made from one hundred percent natural latex and are biodegradable; thus putting Maple City Rubber Company in the forefront of forward-thinking manufacturers.

The vibrant color of Tuf-Tex balloons is on display in this image. The quality and versatility of the Tuf-Tex line makes them the perfect choice for balloon drops and special events.

From the inception of the company to present day there is a sense of community, family and togetherness that binds the employees of Maple City Rubber. Undoubtedly, this family bond has helped sustain Maple City Rubber Company's success thus far and will continue to do so well into the future.

CPSIA information can be obtained at www.ICGtesting.com
Printed in the USA
BVOW10*1234290315

393733BV00002B/2/P